LIFE IN THE
U.S.
COAST GUARD

by Mari Bolte

PEBBLE
a capstone imprint

Published by Pebble, an imprint of Capstone
1710 Roe Crest Drive, North Mankato, Minnesota 56003
capstonepub.com

Copyright © 2025 by Capstone. All rights reserved. No part of this publication may be reproduced in whole or in part, or stored in a retrieval system, or transmitted in any form or by any means, electronic, mechanical, photocopying, recording, or otherwise, without written permission of the publisher.

Library of Congress Cataloging-in-Publication Data is available on the Library of Congress website.

ISBN: 9780756579937 (hardcover)
ISBN: 9780756580308 (paperback)
ISBN: 9780756579951 (ebook PDF)

Summary: Gives readers a peak into daily life for U.S. Coast Guardsmen.

Editorial Credits
Editor: Mandy Robbins; Designer: Heidi Thompson; Media Researcher: Jo Miller; Production Specialist: Tori Abraham

Image Credits
Shutterstock: Andrii Oleksiienko, 21, aviahuisman, 19, Monkey Business Images, 15, Picksell, background (throughout); U.S. Air National Guard photo by Audra Flanagan, 7; U.S. Coast Guard photo by Petty Officer 1st Class Rob Simpson, Cover (top middle), Petty Officer 2nd Class Annie R. B. Elis, 8, 14, Petty Officer 2nd Class Barry Bena, 17, Petty Officer 2nd Class Jetta H. Disco, 18, Petty Officer 2nd Class Ryan L. Noel, 11, Petty Officer 2nd Class Tara Molle, Cover, (bottom), Petty Officer 2nd Class Travis Magee, Cover, (top left), Petty Officer 3rd Class Alejandro Rivera, Cover, (top right), Petty Officer 3rd Class Christopher M. Yaw, 5, Petty Officer 3rd Class Corinne Zilnicki, 9, Photo by Petty Officer 1st Class Levi Read, 13,

The appearance of U.S. Department of Defense (DoD) visual information does not imply or constitute DoD endorsement.

Any additional websites and resources referenced in this book are not maintained, authorized, or sponsored by Capstone. All product and company names are trademarks™ or registered® trademarks of their respective holders.

TABLE OF CONTENTS

Keeping the Coasts Safe 4

Where In the World? 6

On the Job 12

Coast Guard Way of Life 16

Guard Your Own Coast 20

    Glossary 22

    Read More 23

    Internet Sites 23

    Index 24

    About the Author 24

Words in **bold** appear in the glossary.

KEEPING THE COASTS SAFE

The U.S. Coast Guard protects the land and sea. **Ports**, waterways, and **harbors** are safe thanks to them.

Sometimes, boaters need help. Ships sink. People fall into the water. Ice blocks the way. The Coast Guard saves the day!

WHERE IN THE WORLD?

Many military service members live on **bases** or ships. But the Coast Guard is different. Although they work near water, most Coast Guard members live on land. Not everyone serves near the ocean. Rivers and lakes need the Coast Guard too.

Coast Guard members are on every **continent**. They sail across every sea to protect American interests.

People who need the Coast Guard's help can use a special radio channel. There are also phone numbers for local emergencies.

Both men and women are called Coast Guardsmen. They get a new assignment every two to four years. They move to new cities.

Coast Guardsmen might serve on patrol ships called cutters. They leave their families behind on land. Cutters are at sea between one week and three months.

Cutters watch for people breaking the law. Sometimes, just seeing a cutter stops people from acts of crime.

ON THE JOB

Guardsmen have many different jobs. Cutters have weapons. Someone must make sure they are always ready. Someone needs to drive the cutter too.

There are also other ways to keep people safe. Divers must swim in rough water. Helicopter pilots look for lost ships at sea.

Not everyone in the Coast Guard serves on the water. **Intelligence** specialists look for threats. They make sure they have all the information before a mission even begins. Electronics technicians work on computers. Other people fix ships or planes.

Coast Guard families might need help moving. Someone is there to make sure they have what they need.

COAST GUARD WAY OF LIFE

The Coast Guard's **motto** is "Semper Paratus." That means "Always Ready." The Coast Guard saves boaters in trouble. They stop crime and help clean up oil spills.

The Coast Guard is commanded by the Department of Homeland Security. During times of war, it is often put under control of the Navy.

Coast Guardsmen help clean up an oil spill.

Joining the Coast Guard is one way to see the world. Traveling can make life fun and interesting!

After their service is complete, guardsmen leave with valuable skills. They can find a job they like. Some even go back to school. Their education is paid for by the Coast Guard.

GUARD YOUR OWN COAST

Create your own coast to protect. Use sidewalk chalk to draw a body of water. Draw and cut out pictures of boats, people, and even helicopters.

You can move your boats around. Has a person fallen overboard? Use a Coast Guard boat or a helicopter to rescue them!

GLOSSARY

base (BAYS)—an area run by the military where people serving in the military live and military supplies are stored

continent (KAHN-tuh-nuhnt)—one of Earth's seven large land masses

harbor (HAR-bur)—a place where ships load and unload passengers and cargo

intelligence (in-TEL-uh-jenss)—secret information about an enemy's plans or actions

motto (MOTT-oh)—a short sentence that tells what someone believes in or stands for

pilot (PYE-luht)—a person who flies a helicopter or airplane

port (PORT)—a harbor where ships dock safely

READ MORE

Bolte, Mari. *Warships in Action*. Minneapolis: Lerner Publications, 2024.

London, Martha. *US Coast Guard Equipment and Vehicles*. Minneapolis: Kids Core, an imprint of Abdo Publishing, 2022.

Mason, Jenny. *U.S. Coast Guard*. Minneapolis: Kaleidoscope, 2023.

INTERNET SITES

Britannica Kids: Coast Guard
kids.britannica.com/students/article/coast-guard/273712

Operation Military Kids
operationmilitarykids.org/coast-guard/

USO: What Does the Coast Guard Do and 7 Coast Guard Facts to Know
uso.org/stories/2799-what-does-the-coast-guard-do-and-7-coast-guard-facts-to-know

INDEX

assignments, 10

bases, 6
boaters, 4, 16

crime, 10, 16
cutters, 10, 12

Department of Homeland Security, 16

education, 19
emergencies, 4, 9

families, 10, 15

harbors, 4

jobs, 12, 14, 19

motto, 16
moving, 10, 15

ports, 4

radio channels, 9

weapons, 12

ABOUT THE AUTHOR

Mari Bolte is the author and editor of hundreds of children's books. Every book is her favorite book as long as the readers learned something and enjoyed themselves!